THE ULTIMATE INDIANAPOLIS COLTS TRIVIA BOOK

A Collection of Amazing Trivia Quizzes and Fun Facts for Die-Hard Colts Fans!

Ray Walker

978-1-953563-47-7

Exclusive Free Book

Crazy Sports Stories

As a thank you for getting a copy of this book I would like to offer you a free copy of my book Crazy Sports Stories which comes packed with interesting stories from your favorite sports such as Football, Hockey, Baseball, Basketball and more.

Grab your free copy over at

RayWalkerMedia.com/Bonus

CONTENTS

INTRODUCTION

Obviously, you're inspired by your favorite team. In this case, the team in lights is none other than the Indianapolis Colts. The team began in Baltimore in 1953, joined the new AFC in 1970, and has surely been one of the best ever in the entire history of the NFL. (Although, archrival New England Patriots fans might want to argue over your claim just a bit.)

The city of Indianapolis, "the Crossroads of America," has always been the home to exciting sports and winning pro teams: the Indianapolis 500 car race, the Indiana Pacers in the NBA, and now the Fever in the WNBA. Major companies in finance, health care, insurance, and trade make the city even more dynamic.

But your Indianapolis Colts are extra special. There's no place in the world to play and watch football like their unique home stadium, Lucas Oil Stadium (also called "The House that Manning Built"), in the middle of downtown Indianapolis—especially when it's filled with 67,000 raucous Colts fans.

Next year, the Colts will celebrate 68 years of existence at (or near!) the peak of the pro football world, and you'll be there, armed with all the trivia and fun facts on their colorful players, big signings and trades, and the incredibly emotional highs and lows of a pro sports team. The Colts have had more than their fair share, including the team's heartbreaking playoff loss in 2004. But we all must overcome, and there are many merrier moments like their magical runs to the Super Bowl in 1971, 2006-07, and 2009-10.

Clearly, you may use the book as you wish. Each chapter contains 20 quiz questions in a mix of multiple-choice and true-false formats, an answer key (Don't worry, it's on a separate page!), and a section of 10 "Did You Know?" factoids about the team.

For the record, the information and stats in this book are current up to the beginning of 2021. The Indianapolis Colts will surely break more records and win more awards as the seasons march on, so keep this in mind when you're watching the next game with your friends. You never quite know: Someone could suddenly start a conversation with the phrase, "Did you know…?" And you'll be ready.

CHAPTER 1:

ORIGINS & HISTORY

QUIZ TIME!

1. What city did the Colts play in before moving to Baltimore in 1953?
    a. Boston
    b. Dallas
    c. Denver
    d. Houston
2. Which illustrious coach did the Colts sign in 1954?
    a. Weeb Ewbank
    b. George Halas
    c. Tom Landry
    d. Don Shula
3. What team did the Colts beat in the 1958 Championship Game called "the Greatest Game Ever Played"?
    a. Chicago Bears
    b. Cleveland Browns

c. New York Giants
d. New York Jets

4. The aforementioned game was "likely the single most important moment in the popularization of professional football in the latter half of the 20th century."

   a. True
   b. False

5. In 1969, the heavily favored Colts faced the upstart New York Jets in the championship game. What was the Jets' brash young quarterback's nickname?

   a. Hammerin' Hank
   b. Broadway Joe
   c. Joltin' Joe
   d. Johnny U

6. How many points were the Colts favored by in that particular game (before they lost, 16-7)?

   a. 8
   b. 10
   c. 18
   d. 21

7. In what year did the Colts (then in Baltimore) finally win their first Super Bowl versus the Dallas Cowboys?

   a. 1970
   b. 1971
   c. 1973
   d. 1975

8. When Colt Alan Ameche scored the winning points on a one-yard run in the 1958 championship, what was that type of game then called?

   a. Golden-goal
   b. Sudden-death
   c. Sudden-victory
   d. Winner-takes-all

9. The team known as the Dallas Texans would only be allowed to move to Baltimore in 1953 if a certain number of season tickets were sold. In six weeks, how many tix did the franchise need to sell?

   a. 8,000
   b. 12,000
   c. 15,000
   d. 25,000

10. Who became the principal owner of the Baltimore Colts in January 1953?

    a. Robert Irsay
    b. Gino Marchetti
    c. Keith Molesworth
    d. Carroll Rosenbloom

11. What famous Baltimore horse race did the name "Colts" come from?

    a. Belmont Stakes
    b. Kentucky Derby
    c. Preakness Stakes
    d. Royal Ascot

12. The Baltimore Colts were one of the first NFL teams to have cheerleaders, a marching band, and a team "fight song."

    a. True
    b. False

13. The Colts can actually be traced to Dayton, Ohio, where they played as the Triangles. Which rival team did they beat in what's considered the first-ever NFL game in 1920?

    a. Canton Bulldogs
    b. Cleveland Tigers
    c. Columbus Panhandles
    d. Miami Seahawks

14. Who was the fan who won the public naming contest in 1947 and chose the Baltimore Colts moniker?

    a. Charles Evans
    b. Mick James
    c. Dan Topping
    d. Adam Vinatieri

15. Where did the Colts play between 1984 and 2007?

    a. Four Winds Field
    b. Hoosier Dome
    c. RCA Dome
    d. Victory Field

16. Since relocating to Indianapolis in 1984, how many times have the Colts won the Super Bowl?

    a. 1
    b. 2

c. 3
d. 4

17. In 1953, Carroll Rosenbloom was awarded what remained of a team called the Dallas Texans. What was that team's prior name in 1944?

    a. Akron Animals
    b. Boston Yanks
    c. Houston Hawks
    d. New York Yankees

18. The 1958 NFL Championship Game, won by the Colts, was seen by a TV audience of about 5 million people.

    a. True
    b. False

19. When the Colts beat Dallas in Super Bowl V (the first after the AFL-NFL merger in 1970), who kicked the winning field goal with five seconds left?

    a. Don McCafferty
    b. Art Modell
    c. Jim O'Brien
    d. Matt Snell

20. When Rosenbloom traded the Colts to Robert Irsay in 1972, what team did he receive in return?

    a. Los Angeles Dodgers
    b. Los Angeles Rams
    c. Oakland Raiders
    d. San Diego Chargers

QUIZ ANSWERS

1. B – Dallas
2. A – Weeb Ewbank
3. C – New York Giants
4. A – True
5. B – Broadway Joe (Namath)
6. C – 18
7. B – 1971
8. B – Sudden-death
9. C – 15,000
10. D – Carroll Rosenbloom
11. C – Preakness Stakes
12. A – True
13. C – Columbus Panhandles
14. A – Charles Evans
15. C – RCA Dome
16. A – 1
17. B – Boston Yanks
18. B – False (The game was seen by 45 million.)
19. C – Jim O'Brien
20. B – Los Angeles Rams

DID YOU KNOW?

1. There were two separate teams with the same name—the "Baltimore Colts"—before 1953. One was disbanded, and the other played on.
2. The turning point for the "new" Colts came in 1954 with the hiring of Coach Weeb Ewbank and quarterback Johnny Unitas ("Johnny U") in 1956. The latter became one of football's all-time greatest quarterbacks.
3. When the New York Jets and Joe Namath managed to clip the Colts in 1969, it was called "the biggest upset in Super Bowl history."
4. In 1984, team owner Robert Irsay failed to get local government funds for a new stadium. He then relocated the team to Indianapolis in the middle of the night before most Colts fans even knew that a move was planned.
5. Even after the franchise left the city, the Colts Marching Band kept the team's spirit alive in Baltimore by playing in parades and at civic events until 1996, when the Cleveland Browns moved into town and became the Ravens.
6. When the Colts set up shop in Indianapolis, they qualified for the playoffs only once in their first 11 seasons in Indy.
7. When NFL Commissioner Bert Bell challenged the city of Baltimore to sell 15,000 season tickets within six weeks in 1953, the sale took only four weeks, and the team was confirmed.

8. From 1953 until 1983, the Colts called Memorial Stadium in Baltimore their humble home.
9. The Colts were named after the famous thoroughbred horse race, the Preakness Stakes, run in Baltimore since 1873 and part of the historic "Triple Crown" series (along with the Kentucky Derby and Belmont Stakes).
10. The Colts finally broke through to win it all in 1958 behind Johnny Unitas, Lenny Moore, and Raymond Berry. They turned right around and did it again in 1959, galloping past the Giants in the NFL Championship Game.

CHAPTER 2:

NUMBERS GAME

QUIZ TIME!

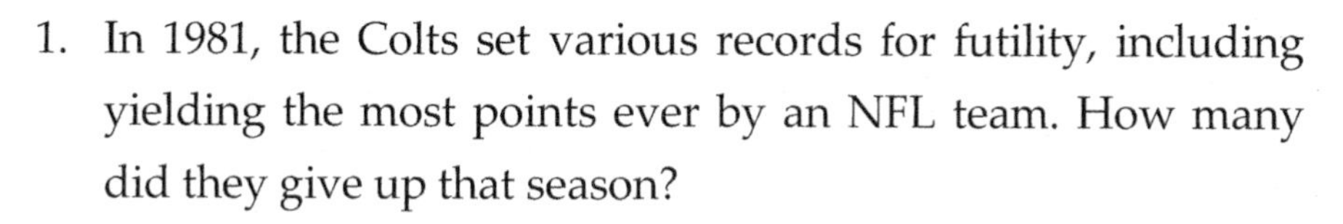

1. In 1981, the Colts set various records for futility, including yielding the most points ever by an NFL team. How many did they give up that season?

    a. 469
    b. 501
    c. 533
    d. 567

2. During that same dire season, the Colts also cracked a modern NFL record with the fewest punt returns by any team ever. How many did they return?

    a. 12
    b. 15
    c. 18
    d. 24

3. After the Colts snuck off to Indianapolis, Unitas declared his allegiance to the new Baltimore team, the Ravens. Only one

other quarterback, Scott Mitchell, ever wore Johnny's number 19 in one season, 1999.

a. True
b. False

4. When Peyton Manning led the Colts to a Super Bowl victory in 2006, how many consecutive seasons of drought ended?

a. 26
b. 30
c. 33
d. 36

5. Manning liked to air it out when he quarterbacked the Colts. How many career passing yards did he put up in 12 years?

a. 50,502
b. 52,367
c. 54,828
d. 56,775

6. In 2019, the financial value of the Colts franchise was divulged. How much was it at that point?

a. $1.8 billion
b. $2.2 billion
c. $2.7 billion
d. $24 billion

7. Speaking of cold hard cash, what was the Colts' average revenue in 2018?

a. $275 million
b. $393 million

c. $510 million
d. $676 million

8. What was the Colts' average home attendance in 2019?

a. 54,337
b. 57,575
c. 61,110
d. 65,666

9. As of 2020, the Colts have a total of 324,000 fans and followers on Facebook and Twitter.

a. True
b. False

10. In 2019, what was the total amount of money the Indianapolis Colts spent on player salaries?

a. $124 million
b. $165 million
c. $238 million
d. $265 million

11. Edgerrin James far exceeds any other Colts runner in career rushing yards. How many yards did he gain?

a. 5,194
b. 5,487
c. 9,226
d. 10,105

12. Who is the Colts' all-time leader in touchdowns, with 128?

a. Marvin Harrison
b. Don McCauley

c. Lenny Moore
d. Reggie Wayne

13. From 1953 to 2020, which of the following Colts' receivers did NOT have more than 5,800 yards receiving?

    a. Raymond Berry
    b. Dallas Clark
    c. T.Y. Hilton
    d. Reggie Wayne

14. In 1966, the Colts' defense "fell asleep" and gave up the longest touchdown pass in franchise history: 99 yards from Karl Sweetan to Pat Studstill. What opponent did they play for?

    a. Chicago Bears
    b. Cleveland Browns
    c. Detroit Lions
    d. Seattle Seahawks

15. No Colts player ever rushed for 100+ yards per game more than Edgerrin James, who managed the feat 49 times. Hall-of-Famer Eric Dickerson is second with 24.

    a. True
    b. False

16. Peyton Manning had more than double the number of 300-yard passing games than the quarterback who's second on the list, Johnny Unitas. Who's third?

    a. Bert Jones
    b. Andrew Luck

c. Earl Morrall
d. Curtis Painter

17. At one point, the Colts had won 15 of 16 games against a certain team. Which was that hapless foe?

a. Houston Texans
b. Miami Dolphins
c. New York Giants
d. New York Jets

18. In 1970, the Colts were one of three NFL teams that joined the AFL's 10 teams to form the fledgling American Football Conference. How much were they paid for this voluntary action?

a. $500,000
b. $1 million
c. $3 million
d. $7.5 million

19. Classy kicker Adam Vinatieri was the first kicker to ever play in five Super Bowls. How many of those did he and his team win?

a. 1
b. 2
c. 4
d. 5

20. In 1999, the Indianapolis Colts became the first team to ever win 11 more games than they had the previous year.

a. True
b. False

QUIZ ANSWERS

1. C – 533
2. A – 12
3. A – True
4. D – 36
5. C – 54,828
6. C – $2.7 billion
7. B – $393 million
8. C – 61,110
9. B – False (They have 3.24 million fans and followers on Facebook and Twitter.)
10. C – $238 million
11. C – 9,226
12. A – Marvin Harrison
13. B – Dallas Clark
14. C – Detroit Lions
15. A – True
16. A – Bert Jones
17. A – Houston Texans
18. C – $3 million

19. C – 4

20. B – False (In 1999, they became the first team ever to win 10 more games than they had the previous year.)

DID YOU KNOW?

1. Carl Taseff was the first player in NFL history to return a missed field goal attempt for a touchdown while with the Colts. He did it twice, in 1956 and 1959.
2. Former Colts quarterback Bert Jones departed from Louisiana State University as their leading career passer, even though he started only 15 games for the Tigers.
3. In 1970, Johnny Unitas became the first player to ever win the NFL Man of the Year Award. This prize is now known as the Walter Payton NFL Man of the Year Award.
4. Along with the Dallas Cowboys' Roger Staubach and the Oakland Raiders' Kenny Stabler, the Colts' Bert Jones was among only three quarterbacks to maintain a passer rating of 100+ during the decade of the 1970s.
5. Until 1968, the Colts' Earl Morrall played for 12 whole years as a backup quarterback for four other teams. Suddenly, Johnny U went down injured, and Morrall stepped in to help the Colts reach the Super Bowl.
6. Bert Jones's longest throw in the air was measured at a "mere" 95 yards.
7. After enjoying his retirement for eight years, Bert Jones decided to lace on his football shoes again at the age of 39 in 1990 to compete in the NFL Quarterback Challenge. He won the "Retirement Division" and went on to finish third versus regular starting quarterbacks.

8. Hall of Fame kicker and quarterback George Blanda played pro football for 27 seasons, one of which (1959) he spent as a kicker with the Colts.
9. As head coach of the Indianapolis Colts, Tony Dungy, and his friend Lovie Smith of the Chicago Bears, became the first two African-American head coaches to guide their teams to the Super Bowl. Then, Dungy became the first African-American head coach in NFL history to win it all.
10. In 2001, Colts running back Dominic Rhodes became the first undrafted player to rush for 1,000+ yards in his rookie campaign.

CHAPTER 3:

CALLING THE SIGNALS

QUIZ TIME!

1. Jim Harbaugh spent seven years with the Bears and ended up in Indianapolis for four more seasons. What was his record as the Colts' starting quarterback?

   a. 34-12
   b. 27-19
   c. 20-26
   d. 15-31

2. In 1995, the Colts advanced to the AFC championship game, where they slipped up against the Steelers. Which Colts receiver was unable to grab a last-second Hail Mary pass by Harbaugh?

   a. Aaron Bailey
   b. Bill Brooks
   c. Jessie Hester
   d. Floyd Turner

3. Along with 122 touchdowns and 101 interceptions, how many yards did Bert Jones pass for in his nine seasons as a Colt?

    a. 12,554
    b. 14,101
    c. 17,663
    d. 20,015

4. One famous coach said that Jones would be on his shortlist to start a franchise with. Who was he?

    a. Bill Belichick
    b. Mike McCarthy
    c. Andy Reid
    d. Ron Rivera

5. When Peyton Manning missed the 2011 season due to injury, the Colts were able to draft one of the best college quarterbacks available, Andrew Luck. Which was his alma mater?

    a. Oklahoma State University
    b. Penn State University
    c. Stanford University
    d. Syracuse University

6. Despite Luck's outstanding ability as a quarterback, he was plagued by injuries. What surgery caused him to miss the entire 2017 season?

    a. Ankle
    b. Elbow

c. Kidney
d. Shoulder

7. How many times was Luck sacked in his 86 games?

a. 96
b. 134
c. 152
d. 174

8. At one point, Colts star quarterback Johnny Unitas threw a touchdown pass in 47 straight games, a record that stood for 52 years. Which quarterback finally broke the record in 2012?

a. Tom Brady
b. Drew Brees
c. Patrick Mahomes
d. Aaron Rodgers

9. An NFL legend, Johnny U tried to make it as a Pittsburgh Steeler but was cut. A friend later persuaded him to leave his construction job to try out with the Baltimore Colts.

a. True
b. False

10. Consistently heralded as one of the NFL's all-time greatest players, what was Johnny's middle name?

a. Christos
b. Constance
c. Constantine
d. Vassilis

11. Unitas led the Colts to three championships, two that were pre-merger and Super Bowl V. How many times was he voted to the Pro Bowl?

    a. 3
    b. 5
    c. 8
    d. 10

12. When he was younger, Unitas dreamed of playing for the Notre Dame Fighting Irish (despite his Lithuanian roots). However, ND coach Frank Leahy said he was simply too skinny and would "get murdered" if put on the field.

    a. True
    b. False

13. Peyton Manning is considered by some the greatest passer in the history of the game. However, how many times was he picked off in his rookie year?

    a. 16
    b. 19
    c. 28
    d. 33

14. Peyton is the son of another famous quarterback, Archie, and has a brother, Eli, who starred for the New York Giants. Why is Peyton's nickname "The Sheriff"?

    a. Due to his ability to audible at the line of scrimmage
    b. Due to the fact that he's never received a speeding or traffic ticket

c. Due to the fact that he always calls teammates the night before a game
d. Due to his part acting in a Western movie

15. During his time in Indy, Manning led the Colts to eight division championships, two AFC championships, and a victory in Super Bowl XLI—the franchise's first in 30 years. With what other team did he later win the Super Bowl?

    a. Arizona Cardinals
    b. Atlanta Falcons
    c. Denver Broncos
    d. Green Bay Packers

16. In how many seasons did Manning pass for more than 4,000 yards?

    a. 7
    b. 10
    c. 12
    d. 14

17. Peyton was one of the most heavily recruited high school players in the nation in 1993, tailed by some 60 schools. Which of the following did NOT actively recruit him?

    a. Connecticut
    b. Florida
    c. Ole Miss
    d. Tennessee

18. After playing for the Colts (and four other pro teams), quarterback Earl Morrall was picked up on waivers by Don

Shula and the Miami Dolphins in 1972. How much was the waiver fee?

a. $100
b. $1,000
c. $10,000
d. $50,000

19. When quarterback Jacoby Brissett was acquired from the Patriots as a backup for Andrew Luck in 2017, who was the Colts' player traded away?

a. Phillip Dorsett
b. Trey Griffey
c. Brad Kaaya
d. Scott Tolzien

20. Peyton Manning once said, "The most valuable player is the one that makes the most players ________." What's missing?

a. Comfortable
b. Happy
c. Money
d. Valuable

QUIZ ANSWERS

1. C – 20-26
2. A – Aaron Bailey
3. C – 17,663
4. A – Bill Belichick
5. C – Stanford University
6. D – Shoulder
7. D – 174
8. B – Drew Brees
9. A – True
10. C – Constantine
11. D – 10
12. A – True
13. C – 28
14. A – Due to his ability to audible at the line of scrimmage
15. C – Denver Broncos
16. D – 14
17. A – Connecticut
18. A – $100
19. A – Phillip Dorsett
20. D – Valuable

DID YOU KNOW?

1. When Andrew Luck decided to retire from football at the relatively young age of 29, he said, "I've been stuck in this process. I haven't been able to live the life I want to live. It's taken the joy out of this game. The only way forward for me is to remove myself from football. This is not an easy decision. It's the hardest decision of my life. But it is the right decision for me."
2. During an interview in 1989, Earl Morrall was asked what it took to leave the bench and become an effective quarterback and team leader. His simple response was: "When you get the chance to do the job, you have to do the job. That's all there is to it."
3. Philip Rivers led the San Diego Chargers to the playoffs six times while taking the Colts there for his seventh playoff appearance. However, his playoff record is 5-7, and he still hasn't reached the Super Bowl.
4. Rivers ranks as the fifth-best quarterback of all time in terms of passing yards (64,440) and touchdowns (421). Both marks are the best for a quarterback who never made it to the Super Bowl.
5. The Colts traded to get a shot at Jeff George in the 1990 Draft. He signed for $15 million, the richest rookie contract ever at that time. George had only one winning season in three with Indy.

6. Johnny Unitas apparently always knew he had what it took. "Conceit is bragging about yourself. Confidence means you believe you can get the job done."
7. Unitas was also recruited by film director Oliver Stone to play one of the opposing football coaches in the 1999 movie *Any Given Sunday*.
8. In 2007, Manning became the first quarterback to beat all the other 31 teams in the NFL in his career when he took the Colts past the Carolina Panthers in Week 8.
9. When the league permanently suspended Colts' quarterback Art Schlichter for gambling in 1983, he was the first to fall for such behavior in 20 years. Paul Hornung and Alex Karras were suspended for the same in 1963.
10. Washington football star John Riggins, himself known for toughness, said that Bert Jones was "the toughest competitor" he had ever witnessed.

CHAPTER 4:

BETWEEN THE TACKLES

QUIZ TIME!

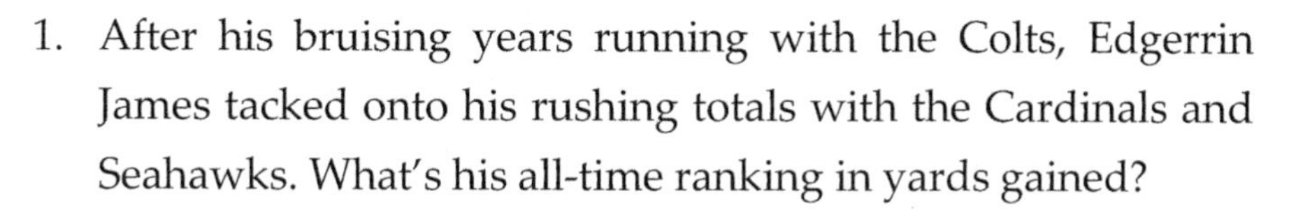

1. After his bruising years running with the Colts, Edgerrin James tacked onto his rushing totals with the Cardinals and Seahawks. What's his all-time ranking in yards gained?

   a. 3rd
   b. 5th
   c. 9th
   d. 13th

2. James ran for more than 1,500+ yards in four seasons as a Colt. In how many of those seasons did he rush for more than 2,000+ yards?

   a. 1
   b. 2
   c. 3
   d. 4

3. In addition to all the yards James churned out in Indy, how many all-purpose touchdowns did he score?

a. 42
b. 51
c. 65
d. 75

4. Marshall Faulk ran like a horse during his time with the Colts. But his trade allowed James to show his stuff. What team was Faulk traded to?

   a. Cincinnati Bengals
   b. Philadelphia Eagles
   c. San Diego Chargers
   d. St. Louis Rams

5. In his first four seasons as a Colt, Faulk rushed for more than 1,000 yards in each. In 1998, his fifth and final year, he sprinted for more than 2,000 yards.

   a. True
   b. False

6. When Marshall moved on to play for the Rams, he helped the team reach two Super Bowls. What was the nickname of that St. Louis juggernaut?

   a. The Greatest Show on Turf
   b. The Fastest Football Show Ever
   c. The Rams Will Rock You
   d. The St. Louis Speedway

7. Lydell Mitchell strutted his stuff with the Colts in the 1970s. He even played on the 1971 Super Bowl team.

a. True
b. False

8. At that time, the NFL schedule was only 14 games. How many all-purpose touchdowns did Mitchell account for in the 1975 season?

    a. 10
    b. 13
    c. 15
    d. 18

9. He played college ball with the Penn State Nittany Lions and many thought the Pittsburgh Steelers would draft Mitchell. But they selected Lydell's famous teammate instead. Who was he?

    a. Rocky Bleier
    b. Franco Harris
    c. Jack Lambert
    d. Lynn Swann

10. Lenny Moore ran the ball for the Colts from 1956 to 1967. His 113 all-purpose touchdowns ranks second on the all-time franchise list. Who's first?

    a. Cary Blanchard
    b. Marvin Harrison
    c. Toni Linhart
    d. Reggie Wayne

11. Born in Pennsylvania, Moore's athleticism and blazing speed earned him numerous nicknames. Which of the following was NOT one of them?

a. Lightning Lenny
b. The Reading Roadrunner
c. The Reading Rocket
d. Sputnik

12. Joseph Addai helped the Colts grab their second Super Bowl title in 2007, their first since 1971. How many total yards did Addai rack up in that Bowl win?

a. 111
b. 130
c. 143
d. 166

13. On November 26, 2006, Addai tied a franchise record by rambling for four touchdowns in a game against the Philadelphia Eagles. Which of the following Colts runners does NOT share this record?

a. Eric Dickerson
b. Frank Gore
c. Lydell Mitchell
d. Lenny Moore

14. During Eric Dickerson's monster season with the Colts in 1988, how many yards per game did he average on the ground?

a. 95
b. 99.9
c. 103.7
d. 107.1

15. Dickerson still holds the all-time single-season NFL rushing record, with 2,405 yards.

    a. True
    b. False

16. Dickerson played with another outstanding recruit and running back, Craig James, while at Southern Methodist University in 1979. What was the nickname given to the dynamic SMU offense?

    a. The Magnificent Mustangs
    b. The Marvelous Mustangs
    c. The Pony Express
    d. The Two-Pronged Pony

17. Alan Ameche was a fantastic fullback for the Colts, famous for scoring the winning touchdown in overtime to beat the Giants in the 1958 Championship Game. Who did he found the Gino's hamburger chain with?

    a. Gino Cappelletti
    b. Gino Marchetti
    c. Gino Marley
    d. Gino Vannelli

18. After Ameche scored the OT clincher to beat the Giants, there wasn't another overtime touchdown scored in championship history until James White of the New England Patriots crossed the line to beat the Falcons, 34-28. In what year?

    a. 1997
    b. 2007

c. 2013
d. 2017

19. After tearing up the turf for the San Francisco 49ers for years, Frank Gore signed a three-year deal worth $12.5 million with the Colts in 2015. How much of this money was guaranteed?

    a. $4 million
    b. $6.5 million
    c. $8.5 million
    d. $10 million

20. In Gore's 2016 season with the Colts, he tied an NFL record for most consecutive seasons (11) with at least five touchdowns. Which of the following players did NOT share this record?

    a. Cris Carter
    b. Matt Hasselbeck
    c. Terrell Owens
    d. Jerry Rice

QUIZ ANSWERS

1. D – 13th
2. C – 3
3. D – 75
4. D – St. Louis Rams
5. A – True
6. A – The Greatest Show on Turf
7. B – False
8. C – 15
9. B – Franco Harris
10. B – Marvin Harrison
11. B – The Reading Roadrunner
12. C – 143
13. B – Frank Gore
14. C – 103.7
15. B – False (Dickerson holds the all-time single-season NFL rushing record, with 2,105 yards.)
16. C – The Pony Express
17. B – Gino Marchetti
18. D – 2017
19. C – $8.5 million
20. B – Matt Hasselbeck

DID YOU KNOW?

1. While the Colts struggled as a team during Frank Gore's stint, he was a solid rusher, finally making way for newcomer Marlon Mack in 2017. Gore ranks third in NFL career rushing yardage as of the end of the 2020 season.
2. Dominic Rhodes broke the record for rushing yards (1,104) by an undrafted rookie in only nine games. He then rumbled for 100+ yards in Super Bowl XLI as Indy battered the Chicago Bears.
3. Tom Matte not only ground out yards, but he also found the end zone on numerous occasions in his 12 seasons with the Baltimore Colts. He rests at sixth on the all-time rushing leaderboard for the Colts, with 4,646 yards.
4. Even though the Colts were upset by the New York Jets in the 1969 Super Bowl, Matte cracked a rushing record that still stands: highest per-carry average (10.5 yards: 116 yards on 11 carries).
5. Tom Matte followed the lead of Johnny Unitas and others when he "disowned" the Colts after their unexpected, controversial move to Indianapolis "in the middle of the night" in 1984.
6. Albert Bentley had a tough choice: He was drafted both by the USFL's Michigan Panthers (who later merged with the Oakland Invaders) and the Colts in 1984. He started with

Michigan, went to Oakland, and ended up in Indy in 1985.

7. In the 2017 NFL Draft, Marlon Mack became the first running back ever drafted out of the University of South Florida. He was the 15th runner drafted that year.

8. Even though his time with the Colts was limited (2016-18), Robert Turbin founded a football academy in Utah, and set up a foundation, Runnin4U, to research cerebral palsy and multiple sclerosis.

9. In 2019, Nyheim Hines showed his blazing speed by running back two punt returns for touchdowns versus the Carolina Panthers. He was the first player in franchise history to accomplish the feat.

10. Though Jordan Wilkins principally played behind Marlon Mack, he lit up the Detroit Lions for 113 yards and a touchdown in Week 8 of the 2020 season, helping the Colts to a 41-21 win.

CHAPTER 5:

CATCHING THE BALL

QUIZ TIME!

1. For a while, the Colts' receiver with the stickiest hands ever, Marvin Harrison, held an NFL record. Which one was it?
    a. Career receiving yards
    b. Career receptions
    c. Single-season receiving touchdowns
    d. Single-season receptions
2. How many touchdown passes did Harrison haul in during his 12-year Colts career?
    a. 103
    b. 118
    c. 128
    d. 141
3. When Harrison caught his 1,000th NFL pass, he joined only three other elite receivers. Which of these was NOT among them?

a. Tim Brown
b. Cris Carter
c. Jerry Rice
d. Amani Toomer

4. Colts receiver Reggie Wayne played the most games of any player in franchise history (211). Who's second on the list?

   a. Marvin Harrison
   b. Peyton Manning
   c. Julius Peppers
   d. Johnny Unitas

5. In Week 10 of 2009, Wayne caught the winning touchdown with 14 seconds left as the Colts snuck by the Patriots. What was the final score of that famous contest, nicknamed "the 4th-and-2 game"?

   a. 21-20
   b. 28-27
   c. 35-34
   d. 42-40

6. In 1960, when the regular season was only 12 games long, Raymond Berry grabbed every ball in sight. What was his average receiving yardage per game?

   a. 95.5
   b. 100.4
   c. 108.2
   d. 115.3

7. Small and unassuming, Berry's meteoric rise to the Hall of Fame has been called one of football's "__________ stories." What word is missing?

   a. Cinderella
   b. Frankenstein
   c. Incredible
   d. Miracle

8. This Colts receiver goes by the name T.Y. Hilton. What are his first and middle names?

   a. Eugene Marquis
   b. Terrence Yarmouth
   c. Thomas Yannick
   d. Tucker Matthew

9. When Hilton hauled in passes totaling 223 yards in Week 6 against the Houston Texans in 2014, he came up a yard short of Raymond Berry's club record. When did Berry set the mark?

   a. 1955
   b. 1957
   c. 1960
   d. 1967

10. When Jimmy Orr ran routes for Baltimore in the 1968 season, his yards-per-reception (YPR) average was 25.6. In his rookie campaign in 1958, his YPR was 27.6.

   a. True
   b. False

11. What was the nickname for the corner of the end zone in Baltimore's Memorial Stadium where Orr caught many of his touchdowns?

    a. Hot Orr's Corner
    b. Orr's Turf
    c. Orrsville
    d. Sweet Orr City

12. Which receiver was heralded as the first Colt inducted into the "Indianapolis Colts Ring of Honor" on August 22, 1998?

    a. Bill Brooks
    b. Dallas Clark
    c. John Mackey
    d. Sean Salisbury

13. What problem did Roger Carr overcome to turn into a football star at Louisiana Tech?

    a. Agoraphobia (fear of crowds)
    b. Carpal tunnel syndrome
    c. Homesickness
    d. Panic disorder

14. Carr said that the discomfort he felt and showed in his final years in Baltimore resulted from the Colts trading away one of his best friends with whom he had a special chemistry. Who was that player?

    a. Ken Huff
    b. Bert Jones
    c. Frank Kush
    d. Bruce Laird

15. Jim "Bucky" Mutscheller played end on both offense and defense and served as team captain for the 1949 national champions in college football. What team did he start for?

    a. Alabama Crimson Tide
    b. Notre Dame Fighting Irish
    c. Penn State Nittany Lions
    d. Oklahoma Sooners

16. In 1957, Mutscheller led the NFL in the number of touchdown passes received. How many did he have?

    a. 7
    b. 8
    c. 10
    d. 14

17. Glenn Martin Doughty caught passes for Baltimore from 1972 to 1979. He later gave his nickname to a family fun center he built and managed. What was it?

    a. Baltimore Diamond
    b. Joltin' Colt
    c. Rattle & Roll
    d. Shake & Bake

18. In 1979, Doughty walked away from the team for two days, complaining that he was being "downgraded" by coach Ted Marchibroda, continuing an "attitude of racism" that Raymond Berry brought to light the year before.

    a. True
    b. False

19. Sean Dawkins helped pave the way in 1997 for Marvin Harrison to explode in the following seasons. Which of the following teams did he NOT later play for?

    a. Chicago Bears
    b. Jacksonville Jaguars
    c. New Orleans Saints
    d. Seattle Seahawks

20. John Mackey was the first president of the NFL Players Association following the AFL-NFL merger in 1970. What was the name of the plan he pioneered to financially support ex-players requiring living assistance?

    a. Assisted Living Package
    b. 88 Plan
    c. Players Profit Plan
    d. Put Players First

QUIZ ANSWERS

1. D – Single-season receptions (143)
2. C – 128
3. D – Amani Toomer
4. B – Peyton Manning (208)
5. C – 35-34
6. C – 108.2
7. A – Cinderella
8. A – Eugene Marquis
9. B – 1957
10. A – True
11. C – Orrsville
12. A – Bill Brooks
13. C – Homesickness
14. B – Bert Jones
15. B – Notre Dame Fighting Irish
16. B – 8
17. D – Shake & Bake
18. A – True
19. A – Chicago Bears
20. B – 88 Plan

DID YOU KNOW?

1. In 1992, John Mackey was inducted into the NFL Hall of Fame as the second "pure" tight end ever elected, after playing in the Pro Bowl five times.
2. When Mackey requested a trade in 1972, he was placed on waivers. But no team picked him up in a communal effort to "blackball" him for leading the Players Association. He finally signed for one season with the San Diego Chargers and then promptly retired.
3. At Twin River Valley High School in Bode, Iowa, Dallas Clark (future Colts tight end) recorded 160 tackles in his senior year to go along with an MVP award, team captaincy, and all-conference honors.
4. When Clark was chosen in the 1st round of the 2003 Draft, he was dubbed a "perfect fit" for the Colts' system. He soon replaced Marcus Pollard and Ken Dilger at tight end.
5. A member of the 2006 Super Bowl winners, Clark smashed John Mackey's Colts records for tight ends with 55 receptions and 11 touchdowns in 2007.
6. Colts tight end Thomas "The Crocodile" Mitchell became notorious for pouring a pitcher of beer over writer George Plimpton's head—an escapade captured in the book *Mad Ducks and Bears*.

7. In his final game as a senior at Oaks Christian School (CA), Colts draftee Michael Pittman Jr. caught 16 passes for 354 yards and five touchdowns.
8. In a Week 10 win over the Tennessee Titans in 2020, Pittman was the first Colts rookie to have 100+ yards receiving since Donte Moncrief did it in 2014.
9. Jessie Hester caught passes for the Colts from 1990 to 1993. He's also the subject of a book called *Muck City* by Bryan Mealer about Hester's experiences as a high school football coach in Belle Glade, FL.
10. Pierre Garçon was one of Peyton Manning's favorite deep threats in 2009 and 2010. He was also known for his backflips after scoring goals in high school soccer and is fluent in French due to his Haitian ancestry.

CHAPTER 6:

TRENCH WARFARE

QUIZ TIME!

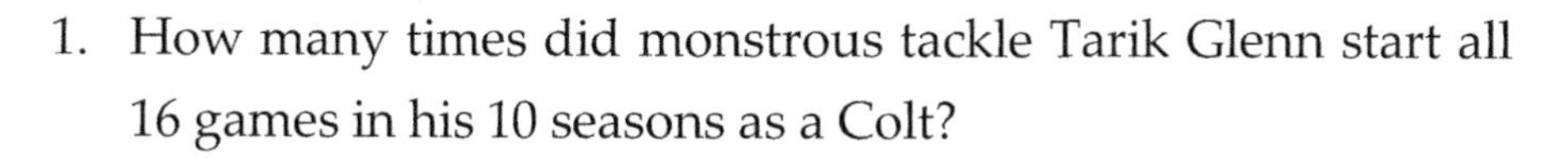

1. How many times did monstrous tackle Tarik Glenn start all 16 games in his 10 seasons as a Colt?
    a. 4
    b. 6
    c. 7
    d. 9
2. On July 24, 2007, soon after winning Super Bowl XLI the previous season, Glenn announced his retirement, saying he'd lost his passion for football.
    a. True
    b. False
3. Offensive lineman Ryan Diem played four seasons for the Northern Illinois University Huskies from 1997-2000. What was his college major?
    a. Drama and theater
    b. Mechanical engineering

c. Physical education
d. Studio art

4. Based solely on his combine workouts, *Pro Football Weekly* surmised that Diem would be a 1st round draft pick. But they also called him "an average athlete with ___________." What word is missing?

a. Brains
b. Limitations
c. Speed
d. Strength

5. Colts center Jeffrey Saturday's high school coach said 80% of the offense was run behind him, yet he was once considered too short to play college ball in the SEC. What's his height?

a. 5 ft. 9 in. (1.75 m)
b. 5 ft. 11 in. (1.80 m)
c. 6 ft. 2 in. (1.88 m)
d. 6 ft. 4 in. (1.93 m)

6. Saturday started at center for the Colts in the 2000 season. How many consecutive game starts did he then reel off?

a. 62
b. 74
c. 85
d. 97

7. When Saturday flattened the Bears' Vince Wilfork to spring the Colts' Joseph Addai for a Super Bowl touchdown, what did he want the play to be called, according to friend and teammate, Peyton Manning?

a. Bowling for Bears
b. Spoon, Knife, and Fork
c. Sweet Redemption
d. The Block

8. In 2006, Gary Brackett was the Colts' defensive captain while he recorded 160 tackles. After his retirement in 2011, he received a master's degree in business administration and opened a series of restaurants, including CharBlue in downtown Indianapolis.

    a. True
    b. False

9. "Big Daddy" Lipscomb was a Colts lineman from 1956 to 1960. What other professional sport did he excel at?

    a. Bowling
    b. Rugby
    c. Softball
    d. Wrestling

10. Robert Mathis was a bruising Colts linebacker and a Super Bowl winner in 2006. In what defensive category is he the all-time NFL career leader?

    a. Forced fumbles
    b. Interceptions
    c. Sacks
    d. Tackles

11. In 1999, Steve McKinney was part of an offensive line for the Colts that yielded a record low number of sacks. How many did this heavyweight gang give up?

a. 13
b. 18
c. 22
d. 28

12. After leaving Indy through free agency in 2002, McKinney was the first unrestricted free agent picked up by a certain team. Which franchise was it?

    a. Arizona Cardinals
    b. Houston Oilers
    c. Houston Texans
    d. Tampa Bay Buccaneers

13. Dwight Freeney played 10 solid seasons for the Colts. In addition to lettering in the traditional sports (football, basketball, and baseball) at Bloomfield (CT) High, what other sport did he play for a year?

    a. Lacrosse
    b. Soccer
    c. Synchronized swimming
    d. Water polo

14. Freeney set a rookie record, forcing nine fumbles during the 2002 season, three of which were against Donovan McNabb in the same game. Which alma mater did Freeney and McNabb share?

    a. Syracuse
    b. University of Michigan
    c. University of Washington
    d. University of Wisconsin

15. Although sacks weren't officially recorded during the era Mike "Mad Dog" Curtis played (1965-78), he had at least 22 of them in his career. He's most famous for a photo showing him tackling a famous quarterback's head. Who was the lucky victim?

    a. Terry Bradshaw
    b. Roman Gabriel
    c. Sonny Jurgensen
    d. Bart Starr

16. Curtis was notorious as a weak-side (away from the tight end) linebacker. But what position was he drafted by the Colts to play?

    a. Halfback
    b. Fullback
    c. Defensive lineman
    d. Tight end

17. Ted "The Mad Stork" Hendricks formed part of a terrifying defensive tandem with Curtis. He was honored as being the first NFL player of his nationality. Which one?

    a. Costa Rican
    b. Guatemalan
    c. Panamanian
    d. El Salvadorean

18. Hendricks used his height (6 ft. 7 in./2.01 m) to block passes and field goals. He also had an unusual number for a linebacker because he started out as a defensive end. What was his number?

a. 79
b. 83
c. 95
d. 101

19. In his prime, Ray May was a mainstay of the 1971 Colts defense that allowed the second fewest points in the NFL. After he retired, he had to fight for the NFL's support due to the numerous surgeries he was forced to undergo.

    a. True
    b. False

20. Duane Bickett was credited by his Colts coaches with having 1,052 career tackles. How many other defenders of the franchise had more than 700?

    a. 4
    b. 6
    c. 9
    d. 13

QUIZ ANSWERS

1. C – 7
2. A – True
3. B – Mechanical engineering
4. B – Limitations
5. C – 6 ft. 2 in. (1.88 m)
6. C – 85
7. D – The Block
8. A – True
9. D – Wrestling
10. A – Forced fumbles (52)
11. C – 22
12. C – Houston Texans
13. B – Soccer
14. A – Syracuse
15. B – Roman Gabriel
16. B – Fullback
17. B – Guatemalan
18. B – 83
19. A – True
20. B – 6

DID YOU KNOW?

1. In 2011, Linebacker Gary Brackett published *Winning: From Walk-On to Captain, In Football and Life*, a memoir, including his achievements and struggles with family, college, and the NFL.
2. Despite never making it to the Hall of Fame in Canton, Gene "Big Daddy" Lipscomb was named to the Hall of Very Good Class of 2006 by the Professional Football Researchers Association.
3. Steve Emtman had a cameo appearance as himself in the 1994 film *Little Giants,* along with Bruce Smith, Tim Brown, Emmitt Smith, and John Madden. He also acted as an uncredited zombie in the TV series *Z Nation*. His son was the zombie baby in the first episode.
4. "Ted (Hendricks) was an octopus. He had arms long enough to reach over blockers and take down ball carriers. Mike (Curtis) just wanted to knock the crap out of you, and after every tackle, he had this John Wayne way of walking back to the huddle," Ray May said, describing his destructive teammates.
5. Buffalo, in particular, felt the wrath of the Colts' swarming defense. In three successive meetings in 1971 and 1972, they blanked the Bills by a combined 84-0.
6. When Ray May arrived in Baltimore after suffering with the then-dismal Steelers, he was full of self-doubts. Johnny

Unitas took him aside and said, "Y'know, Ray, we could have gotten any player on the Steelers, but we got you. Now prove to us that we took the right guy."

7. The opposing player Duane Bickett respected most was Dan Marino: "He had such command and presence on the field. If you made the slightest error in alignment or positioning on coverage, he took advantage. He saw everything on the football field. There was no throw he wouldn't make."

8. Jeff Herrod led the Indianapolis team in tackles seven times during an eight-year stretch starting in 1989.

9. Before the Colts, Barry Krauss played for the legendary Paul "Bear" Bryant at Alabama. Krauss's most famous play occurred in the 1979 Sugar Bowl, stopping Penn State runner Mike Guman short of the goal line late in the last quarter.

10. Former BYU Cougar Rob Morris was the starting middle linebacker for the Colts for his first five seasons, as well as the leading special teams tackler in 2006. He also subbed for Bruce Gardner to improve the Colts' defense against the run, resulting in a Super Bowl win that year.

CHAPTER 7:

NO AIR ZONE

QUIZ TIME!

1. Defensive back Ray Buchanan had a peculiar nickname when he was picking off passes for the Colts from 1993 to 1996. What was it?
   a. Better-Believe Ray
   b. Big-Play Ray
   c. Evil-Way Ray
   d. Ray-In-Your-Eye
2. Along with his nickname "The Sandman," safety Bob Sanders was called "The Eraser" by his Indy coach, Tony Dungy, in 2007. Why?
   a. He erased point deficits with multiple interceptions.
   b. He erased the mistakes of his teammates with timely plays.
   c. His favorite movie was *Eraserhead.*
   d. He made Coach Dungy constantly erase plays that didn't work from the playbook.

3. Safety Bobby Boyd sits in a tie for 13th place on the all-time NFL interception list (with 57 picks in total) with a few individuals. Which of the following players is he NOT tied with?

    a. Mel Blount
    b. Joe Kapp
    c. Eugene Robinson
    d. Everson Walls

4. When Boyd retired in 1969, he joined the Colts' coaching staff and helped take the 1970 squad to the Super Bowl. Who did he eventually go into the restaurant business with?

    a. Ellery Eskelin
    b. Damon Evans
    c. Johns Hopkins
    d. Johnny Unitas

5. Rick Volk, who played safety for Baltimore when they won the 1968 NFL Championship and the 1970 Super Bowl, was chosen by fans as a starter on the Colts' 25th Anniversary Team. In what year was he picked for this honor?

    a. 1975
    b. 1977
    c. 1980
    d. 1986

6. Volk desperately wanted to go to the University of Michigan to follow in the footsteps of his uncle, Bob Chappuis. Also, his grandpa didn't like Woody Hayes, the Ohio State coach,

and apparently hoped that Woody would choke on his Thanksgiving ________. What word is missing?

a. Bowl game
b. Dinner
c. Speech
d. Turkey

7. What did modest Jerry Logan tell reporters was the important element needed to intercept a pass from the likes of Broadway Joe Namath?

   a. Anticipation
   b. Foresight
   c. Keen eyesight
   d. Luck

8. Baltimore's Daniel "Bert" Rechichar, principally a defensive back, was summoned to kick a 56-yard field goal against the Bears, the first of his career. He drilled it, and held the record for longest field goal until the Saints' Tom Dempsey crushed a 62-yarder in 1970, 17 years later.

   a. True
   b. False

9. In their magical run to the 2007 Super Bowl, Indianapolis safety Antoine Bethea ran wild in a 15-6 win at the Baltimore Ravens in the AFC divisional round. Which of the following feats did Bethea NOT do?

   a. Broke up a pass
   b. Intercepted a pass by Steve McNair

c. Joined in on six combined tackles
d. Recovered a fumble

10. Who was the head coach responsible for naming Vontae Davis the starting cornerback in 2012, a season in which Davis had five solo tackles, three deflections, and two picks in one game against Houston?

    a. Lindy Infante
    b. Jim Mora
    c. Chuck Pagano
    d. John Sandusky

11. What record did Colts linebacker Don Shinnick set that still stands to this day?

    a. Career interceptions (37) by a linebacker
    b. Single-season interceptions (9) by a linebacker
    c. Career pass deflections (32) by a linebacker
    d. Single-season pass deflections (10) by a linebacker

12. Outstanding cornerback Milt Davis retired after only four years in the NFL due to his anger at the treatment of black players (including segregated hotels and restaurants). He eventually moved to Oregon to farm with his wife. Which of the following animals did he NOT raise?

    a. Cattle
    b. Llama
    c. Sheep
    d. Spider goats

13. In 1954, Lenny Lyles broke the University of Louisville's color barrier for scholarship athletes. He remains Louisville's all-time leading scorer for a non-kicker, with 300 points.

    a. True
    b. False

14. In 1997, Eugene Daniel notched the longest interception return (97 yards) in the history of the Colts. Who was the sorry opponent on that fateful day?

    a. Baltimore Ravens
    b. New England Patriots
    c. New York Giants
    d. New York Jets

15. Bruce Laird was primarily a strong safety for the Colts. Although he never took back a punt for a touchdown, he amassed multiple yards as a returner. How many did he rack up on 213 attempts in his career?

    a. 2,130
    b. 2,575
    c. 3,487
    d. 3,748

16. After safety Jason Belser endured consecutive 3-13 seasons with the Colts in 1997-98, he admitted, "I realized I couldn't take that __________ home." What word is missing?

    a. Bacon
    b. Beating
    c. Frustration
    d. Pain

17. When Mike Adams re-signed with the Colts at free safety for $4.85 million in 2015, who was his playing partner at strong safety?

    a. Sergio Brown
    b. Dwight Lowery
    c. Corey Lynch
    d. Charlie Whitehurst

18. In 2015, Clayton Geathers was rated the fifth-best safety prospect in the land leading up to the NFL Draft. Which scouting agency provided this rating?

    a. BestDraft.com
    b. DraftScout.com
    c. Draft Your Man Inc.
    d. Scouts Inc.

19. Darius Leonard was ranked as one of the league's best defenders in coverage, regardless of position, in 2020. Which of the following metrics was NOT included in the assessment?

    a. Ballhawk rate
    b. Catch rate allowed below expectation
    c. Coverage-success rate
    d. Rushing efficiency

20. At the 2019 NFL Combine, safety Marvell Tell turned heads with his 42-inch (107 cm) vertical leap. However, on August 5, 2020, Tell announced he would opt out of the coming season due to the COVID-19 crisis.

    a. True
    b. False

QUIZ ANSWERS

1. B – Big-Play Ray
2. B – He erased the mistakes of his teammates with timely plays.
3. B – Joe Kapp
4. D – Johnny Unitas
5. B – 1977
6. D – Turkey
7. D – Luck
8. B – False (Dempsey's kick was actually a 63-yarder.)
9. D – Recovered a fumble
10. C – Chuck Pagano
11. A – Career interceptions (37) by a linebacker
12. D – Spider goats
13. A – True
14. D – New York Jets
15. D – 3,748
16. C – Frustration
17. B – Dwight Lowery
18. B – DraftScout.com
19. D – Rushing efficiency
20. A – True

DID YOU KNOW?

1. As much as Ray Buchanan tried to dissuade his sons from playing football, both Ray Jr. and Baylen insisted on the sport. "I'll do as much as I can to help out but football only provides you a platform. I talk to them all the time to look for what they want to do after football," Ray said.
2. Rather than talk about the Jets' upset of Baltimore in the 1969 Super Bowl, ex-safety Jerry Logan prefers to talk about the revenge game in 1970, when the Colts' secondary intercepted six Namath passes, sacked him three times, and won 29-22.
3. Andy Nelson spent two years as a player and defensive coach with the Harrisburg Capitols of the Atlantic Coast Football League, the Colts' farm team. He led the league in pass defense before being named the head coach. Nelson then became defensive coordinator of the Norfolk Neptunes, winning a league championship in 1971.
4. As proof of Bert Rechichar's toughness in the early '50s, he once quipped to Howard "Hopalong" Cassady (a former Heisman Trophy winner) after tackling him hard near the sidelines, "Listen, Cassady, this ain't Ohio State. This is the National Football League and we tear out your eyeballs."
5. Milt Davis was initially drafted by the Detroit Lions in 1954. But, after he returned from military service, they told him, "We don't have a black teammate for you to go on road trips. Therefore, you can't stay on our team."

6. In the 1958 NFL Championship Game against the New York Giants, Davis forced one of two first-half fumbles by Frank Gifford, both resulting in Colts scores. Davis was playing with two broken bones in his right foot at the time.
7. When Eugene Daniel was drafted by the Colts at cornerback in 1984, he was worried about another corner in front of him, Leonard Coleman. Teammate Tracy Porter said, "Eugene was gravely concerned because Coleman got the plays and publicity. I told him to disregard it and play his game. I told him he had skills and could make the team." Daniel went on for 12 more years and is one of nine Colts with three interceptions in a single game.
8. After the NFL, Bruce Laird played for both the Arizona Outlaws and Arizona Wranglers in the USFL. He stayed active after his career as a member of the Board of Directors of Fourth & Goal, an independent organization to benefit retired NFL players.
9. As the senior director of player affairs and development for the NFL Players Association, Jason Belser said, "I find myself busy making sure the players understand the wages, hours, and working conditions which are negotiated in the collective bargaining agreement."
10. "I know I've gotten better, I've taken strides in the right direction, trying to be the player this defense needs me to be," rookie Khari Willis said while taking over the starting safety spot in 2019.

CHAPTER 8:

SUPER BOWL SALUTE

QUIZ TIME!

1. The 1958 NFL Championship Game, featuring the Baltimore Colts and the New York Giants, was the first ever to be decided in overtime. Where was the game played?
   a. Giants Stadium, New York
   b. Memorial Stadium, Baltimore
   c. The Polo Grounds, New York
   d. Yankee Stadium, New York
2. The so-called "Greatest Game Ever Played" (above) was confirmed again as the best in the league's first 100 years by the media in 2019. How many press members gave it the nod in this nationwide survey?
   a. 44
   b. 55
   c. 66
   d. 81

3. One of the reasons that the NFL eventually rose to the top of the U.S. sports market was this very game, which was shown across the land by NBC.

   a. True
   b. False

4. Raymond Berry hauled in 12 catches (a record that stood for 55 years) for 178 yards and a touchdown in the 1958 Championship. Which Denver Bronco finally broke the record in 2014?

   a. Nathan Palmer
   b. Emmanuel Sanders
   c. Demaryius Thomas
   d. Kyle Williams

5. Back in the NFL Championship Game against the Giants once more in 1959, how many points were the Colts favored by?

   a. 3.5
   b. 6
   c. 9
   d. 14

6. The NFL provided five game officials in 1959. When was the line judge added to the mix?

   a. 1960
   b. 1965
   c. 1978
   d. 1986

7. How much did each of the winning Colts players get as their share for winning in 1959?

   a. $1,888
   b. $4,674
   c. $8,988
   d. $12,425

8. Which two of the following announcers were privileged to call the excitement of the 1959 NFL Championship Game, won by Baltimore (31-16), on NBC?

   a. Howard Cosell and "Dandy Don" Meredith
   b. Bob Costas and Merlin Olsen
   c. Cris Collinsworth and Al Michaels
   d. Chris Schenkel and Chuck Thompson

9. Coming into the 1968 NFL Championship Game, the Colts had just won their division. What was the name of the division at that time?

   a. Atlantic Coast Conference
   b. Coastal Division
   c. Eastern Conference
   d. Mideast Division

10. Besides quarterback Bill Nelsen, who spearheaded the attack of the opponent Cleveland Browns in this 1968 showdown?

    a. Ernie Green
    b. Leroy Kelly
    c. Milt Morin
    d. Paul Warfield

11. It all went quite wrong for the Browns on that day in 1968, even though they were playing at home. They crossed midfield only twice, while Cleveland kicker Don Cockroft missed three field goal attempts. What was the paltry number of total yards Cleveland gained in the game?

    a. 121
    b. 147
    c. 173
    d. 181

12. Who was the massive Colts lineman who blocked one of Cockroft's kicks in the 1968 game?

    a. Bubba Smith
    b. Billy Ray Smith
    c. Ordell Braase
    d. Sudden Sam Smith

13. Where did New York quarterback Joe Namath make his famous appearance three days before the 1969 championship, guaranteeing victory for his underdog Jets?

    a. Copper 29 Bar, Miami
    b. Miami Touchdown Club
    c. NBC Studios, New York
    d. Studio 54, New York

14. Before the 1969 championship game, Weeb Ewbank had coached the Colts, only to be replaced by future legend Don Shula. What was the previous team name of the Jets just before acquiring Ewbank?

a. Dodgers
b. Giants
c. Titans
d. Yankees

15. The shootout in 1969 between the Baltimore Colts and New York Jets was the third NFL championship and the first to officially use the trademark name "Super Bowl."

a. True
b. False

16. Which team did the Colts beat in the AFC championship to get to the 1971 Super Bowl in Miami's Orange Bowl against the Dallas Cowboys?

a. Cincinnati Bengals
b. Miami Dolphins
c. Oakland Raiders
d. San Francisco 49ers

17. How many ticks remained on the game clock when the Colts' Jim O'Brien drilled the field goal to clinch a 16-13 victory over the Cowboys and their vaunted "Doomsday Defense" in the 1971 Bowl?

a. 5 seconds
b. 15 seconds
c. 24 seconds
d. 33 seconds

18. Super Bowl V was the first Super Bowl ever to be carried live in the state of Alaska, thanks to NBC's then-parent company

ESPN acquiring the Alaska Communications System from the United States Air Force.

a. True
b. False

19. Super Bowl XLI in 2007 featured two teams suffering from long Super Bowl droughts. The Colts were back for the first time since 1970. When had the Bears previously competed in the big Bowl?

    a. 1978
    b. 1981
    c. 1985
    d. 1989

20. The Colts' Tony Dungy became the first African-American coach to ever win the biggest NFL game. Where had he coached previously?

    a. New England Patriots
    b. New York Giants
    c. SW Florida Gladiators
    d. Tampa Bay Buccaneers

QUIZ ANSWERS

1. D – Yankee Stadium, New York
2. C – 66
3. A – True
4. C – Demaryius Thomas
5. A – 3.5
6. B – 1965
7. B – $4,674
8. D – Chris Schenkel and Chuck Thompson
9. B – Coastal Division
10. B – Leroy Kelly
11. C – 173
12. A – Bubba Smith
13. B – Miami Touchdown Club
14. C – Titans
15. A – True
16. C – Oakland Raiders
17. A – 5 seconds
18. B – False (NBC's then-parent company was RCA, not ESPN.)
19. C – 1985
20. D – Tampa Bay Buccaneers

DID YOU KNOW?

1. In the 1958 Championship Game, with the Colts driving in OT, someone ran out onto the field at Yankee Stadium, causing a delay in the game. Rumor has it that it was an NBC employee ordered to create a distraction because the national TV feed had gone dead.
2. The Colts' Tom Matte showed off for the "home" crowd in Cleveland in the 1968 championship, rushing for 88 yards and three touchdowns, while also catching two passes for 15 yards. Matte went to Shaw High School in East Cleveland and was a former Ohio State quarterback.
3. Only two teams in NFL history have ever lost by a worse score than the Colts over Cleveland in the 1968 championship (34-0). The Packers crushed the Giants (37-0) in 1961, and the Bears shellacked the Redskins (73-0) in 1940.
4. In 1969, Super Bowl III was the first victory for the AFL in such a championship. Before the contest, the majority of sportswriters and fans believed that AFL teams were less talented than NFL clubs, and expected the Colts to defeat the Jets by a comfortable margin.
5. Broadway Joe Namath was named the most valuable player in the 1969 Super Bowl, making him the first player in the game's history to be declared MVP without personally scoring or passing for a touchdown.

6. Vice President Spiro Agnew, a Colts fan since the team began playing in Baltimore in 1953, attended Super Bowl V in Miami. The former governor of Maryland, he was President Richard Nixon's first vice president. Boxing great Muhammad Ali was also at the game, as he was training nearby for his championship fight in March against "Joltin' Joe" Frazier.
7. Kickoff for Super Bowl V was at 2:00 p.m., making it the earliest start time in the Eastern Time Zone in the game's history and one of only three Bowls to have a morning start for viewers in the Pacific Time Zone (the others were Super Bowl VI in New Orleans and Super Bowl X in Miami).
8. The Super Bowl in 2007 was the first to be played in rainy conditions. The Colts stormed back from a 14-6 first-quarter deficit to outscore the Bears 23-3 in the last three quarters.
9. Colts quarterback Peyton Manning finally won the one that mattered. He was named the game's MVP, completing 25 of 38 passes for 247 yards and a touchdown, against one interception, for a passer rating of 81.8.
10. The CBS broadcast of the 2007 game was caught by an estimated average of 93.2 million viewers, making it, at that time, the fifth-most watched program in U.S. television history. The halftime extravaganza, headlined by rock star Prince, peaked at 140 million.

CHAPTER 9:

SHINING THE BUSTS

QUIZ TIME!

1. After the Colts won Super Bowl XLI, which U.S. president invited them to the White House?
   a. George W. Bush
   b. Jimmy Carter
   c. Bill Clinton
   d. Barack Obama
2. Following the 2002 hiring of head coach Tony Dungy by Colts owner Jim Irsay, in how many consecutive years did the franchise qualify for the playoffs?
   a. 5
   b. 7
   c. 9
   d. 12
3. The Colts hauled in two consecutive Offensive Rookie of the Year Awards in 1955 and 1956. Which players won those awards?

a. Alan Ameche and Lenny Moore
b. Raymond Berry and Jim Parker
c. Rip Collins and Joe Perry
d. Jim Spavital and Y.A. Tittle

4. The Colts won five straight AFC South titles from 2003 to 2007 and racked up seven straight campaigns of 12 or more wins from 2003 to 2009, a first-time occurrence in the 90-year history of the NFL.

   a. True
   b. False

5. "The Golden Arm," Johnny Unitas, won his first Associated Press MVP Award after the 1959 season and was also named the UPI Player of the Year. How many yards did he pass for that season?

   a. 2,544
   b. 2,788
   c. 2,899
   d. 3,113

6. When Unitas won his third MVP award in 1967 with a 58.5 completion percentage, what physical ailment did he openly complain of?

   a. Blurred vision
   b. Dizziness
   c. Tennis elbow
   d. Wobbly knee

7. Don Shula was named NFL Coach of the Year three times in seven seasons with the Colts, from 1963 through 1969. Which of the following successful coaches was on his defensive staff at that time?
   a. Chuck Noll
   b. Hal Hunter
   c. Frank Kush
   d. Howard Schnellenberger
8. Which of the following quarterbacks that Shula coached did NOT make it eventually to the Hall of Fame?
   a. Bob Griese
   b. Dan Marino
   c. Earl Morrall
   d. Johnny Unitas
9. When Ted Marchibroda won the Coach of the Year Award with the Colts, which player won Comeback Player of the Year?
   a. Marshall Faulk
   b. Jim Harbaugh
   c. Bert Jones
   d. Vince Tobin
10. Despite Marchibroda's success with the Colts, both in Baltimore and Indianapolis, he almost retired after less than a season in 1976. What issue did he have with owner Irsay?
   a. The owner physically abused players after a night out.
   b. The owner verbally abused players after a preseason loss.

c. The owner threatened to fire him immediately if he didn't win.
d. The owner threatened to move the team in the middle of the night.

11. In what year did Colts linebacker Vernon Leroy Maxwell win the Defensive Rookie of the Year Award?

a. 1976
b. 1980
c. 1983
d. 1986

12. Even though Colts owner Jim Irsay battled personal demons outside football, he liked to buy "trophies" for himself with some of his spare cash. Which of the following performers' guitars did NOT end up in Irsay's collection?

a. Jerry Garcia
b. John Lennon
c. Elvis Presley
d. Carlos Santana

13. Marshall Faulk was the first player to win both the Offensive Rookie of the Year prize and another significant award in the same campaign (1994). What was the second?

a. FedEx Air & Ground Player of the Year
b. Offensive Player of the Year
c. Pro Bowl MVP
d. Super Bowl MVP

14. One year before Andrew Luck won the NFL Comeback Player of the Year in 2018, he spent more than a month in a foreign country undergoing treatment for his bum shoulder. What was the country?

    a. Belgium
    b. France
    c. Netherlands
    d. Taiwan

15. Peyton Manning holds numerous NFL records, including the most Pro Bowl appearances and the number of seasons in which he passed for 4,000 yards or more—both with the same number. How many?

    a. 9
    b. 11
    c. 13
    d. 14

16. From 2015 to 2016, Adam Vinatieri connected on an NFL record number of consecutive field goals for the Colts. How many times in a row did he split the uprights during that magical phase?

    a. 37
    b. 41
    c. 44
    d. 48

17. Before its debut in 2008, Lucas Oil Stadium was constructed to welcome the Colts. How much of the $720 million needed was provided by the city of Indianapolis and the state of Indiana?

a. $350 million
b. $420 million
c. $550 million
d. $620 million

18. When Bill Polian was hired as Indy president after success with the Bills and then the Panthers, one of his shrewdest moves ever was taking Peyton Manning in the draft rather than another quarterback. Who?

    a. Charlie Batch
    b. Jim Druckenmiller
    c. Ryan Leaf
    d. Jake Plummer

19. When Rodrigo Blankenship booted two field goals and three extra points in a Week 15 win over the Houston Texans in 2020, which kicker did he pass for most extra points as a rookie?

    a. Bucky Dilts
    b. Jim O'Brien
    c. Mike Vanderjagt
    d. Adam Vinatieri

20. When Philip Rivers passed the 60,000-yard mark passing during the 2020 season, which of the following quarterbacks did he NOT join in that elite yardage group?

    a. Tom Brady
    b. Drew Brees
    c. Brett Favre
    d. Joe Montana

QUIZ ANSWERS

1. A – George W. Bush
2. C – 9
3. A – Alan Ameche and Lenny Moore
4. A – True
5. C – 2,899
6. C – Tennis elbow
7. A – Chuck Noll
8. C – Earl Morrall
9. B – Jim Harbaugh
10. B – The owner verbally abused players after a preseason loss.
11. C – 1983
12. D – Carlos Santana
13. C – Pro Bowl MVP
14. C – Netherlands
15. D – 14
16. C – 44
17. D – $620 million
18. C – Ryan Leaf
19. A – Bucky Dilts
20. D – Joe Montana

DID YOU KNOW?

1. By winning Super Bowl XLI, the Colts became the first team that played its home games in a domed stadium ever to win a Super Bowl held in an outdoor stadium.
2. In Marshall Faulk's final year in Indianapolis, before heading off to the Rams, he was the NFL's leader in total yards from scrimmage with an astonishing 2,227. Faulk edged Denver's MVP running back Terrell Davis by a mere two yards.
3. Peyton Manning helped lead both the Colts and Broncos to two Super Bowls and won one with each. He's the only starting quarterback to have multiple appearances and leave the Super Bowl victorious with more than one franchise.
4. Kicker Adam Vinatieri has the most career regular-season wins (215) by a single player in league history. In 2018, Vinatieri hit 23 of 27 field goals (85.2%) and 44 of 47 extra-point attempts (93.6%) for 113 points, marking the 21st 100-point season in his career, extending his NFL record.
5. Whether it won a trophy or not, the Colts' record comeback was when they nipped the Chiefs, 45-44, on January 4, 2014, in the AFC Wild Card game. At one point, the Colts trailed by 28 points.
6. Dwight Freeney was heralded by owner Irsay upon his induction into the Colts Ring of Honor in 2019: "He was an

artist and a terror on the field, and his patented spin move was a nightmare for every offensive lineman he faced. More importantly, he was a leader in the locker room and a gentleman off the field who represented the horseshoe with honor."

7. Though not an NFL record or even a team mark, Kelvin Hayden's 56-yard return on his pick-six of an errant Rex Grossman pass was a career first and a turning point in the Colts' Super Bowl win in 2007.

8. The Ed Block Courage Award is an annual award presented to a player from each NFL team who is voted for by teammates as a role model of inspiration, sportsmanship, and courage. The award is named in memory of Ed Block, a humanitarian and athletic trainer for the Baltimore Colts.

9. When the Colts finally beat the Patriots, 38-34, in a 2006 playoff shootout, their 18-point comeback was the largest ever in an NFL conference championship game and tied the record for the fourth largest NFL post-season comeback.

10. In 2020, Jonathan Taylor (out of Wisconsin) rampaged for 253 yards on the ground in a single game, breaking Edgerrin James's franchise record of 219.

CHAPTER 10:

DRAFT DAY

QUIZ TIME!

1. Peyton Manning is considered by some pundits as the best 1st overall pick in NFL history (with possible competition from Bruce Smith and John Elway). What year was Manning drafted?

    a. 1994
    b. 1996
    c. 1998
    d. 2000

2. Marvin Harrison came to the Colts as their first pick in 1996 and went on to eight Pro Bowls and the Hall of Fame. What was his draft number as an overall pick that year?

    a. 12th
    b. 15th
    c. 19th
    d. 25th

3. Edgerrin James, drafted as the 4th overall pick in 1999, is the latest Colts Hall-of-Famer. His first two seasons were as good as any runner in NFL history, and he recovered from two serious knee injuries to compete in two more Pro Bowls.

    a. True
    b. False

4. Which draft pick was the only other Colt to be named more times as a First Team All-Pro (five times vs. three times) than Dwight Freeney (picked in 2002)?

    a. Tarik Glenn
    b. Peyton Manning
    c. Quenton Nelson
    d. Reggie Wayne

5. The 6th overall pick by the Colts in 2018, Quenton Nelson, did something no other offensive lineman ever did in NFL history. What was his feat?

    a. Allowed no sacks in his first five years
    b. Became the first lineman to start both offensively and defensively
    c. Made First Team All-Pro his first two seasons
    d. Threw a touchdown pass on a trick play in his rookie season

6. Cornelius Bennett was drafted 2nd overall in 1999, but he didn't sign. He was then instrumental in a trade that brought a record-breaking runner to the Colts. Who?

    a. Eric Dickerson
    b. Marshall Faulk

c. Owen Gill
d. Edgerrin James

7. Anthony Salvatore Castonzo was a 1st round Colts pick in the 2011 NFL Draft. As Harvard's right tackle, he protected quarterback Ryan Fitzpatrick and helped account for 5,924 yards in total offense.

a. True
b. False

8. In 2020, it was reported that Colts GM Chris Ballard regularly stated his philosophy: You build teams through the draft. Who was his top pick in 2019?

a. Ben Banogu, TCU
b. Parris Campbell, Ohio State
c. Bobby Okereke, Stanford
d. Rock Ya-Sin, Temple

9. Draftee Dallas Clark was the Colts' "most prolific" all-around tight end. What year was he selected?

a. 2003
b. 2000
c. 1996
d. 1985

10. Jon Thomas Hand was picked 4th overall in 1984. How many times did he start in his 121 career games, all with the Colts?

a. 85
b. 101

c. 110
d. 118

11. Drafted in the 1st round as the 18th overall pick in 2016, what position did Ryan Patrick Kelly start in?

 a. Center
 b. Defensive tackle
 c. Offensive guard
 d. Punter

12. Ron Solt was drafted by the Colts as the 19th overall selection in the 1st round of the 1984 Draft. Which player forced the trade for this pick by refusing to play in Baltimore?

 a. Lynn Dickey
 b. John Elway
 c. Steve Grogan
 d. Tommy Kramer

13. From Texas A&M, linebacker Quentin Coryatt was drafted with the Colts' 2nd overall pick in the 1992 Draft. He became the first "Crucian" (a native of St. Croix, an island in the Caribbean) to play in the NFL.

 a. True
 b. False

14. Which university did the 1st overall pick in 1992, Steve Emtman, help lead to an undefeated season in 1991?

 a. Idaho State University
 b. University of Oregon

c. University of Washington
d. Washington State University

15. The Colts selected safety Malik Hooker in the 1st round with the 15th overall pick in 2017. Which other safety was ranked higher and drafted ahead of Hooker?

    a. Jamal Adams of LSU
    b. Myles Garrett of Texas A&M
    c. Solomon Thomas of Stanford
    d. Mitchell Trubisky of North Carolina

16. The Colts selected Sean Dawkins in the 1st round of the 1993 Draft. With which other team did he enjoy his best season in 1999?

    a. Jacksonville Jaguars
    b. Minnesota Vikings
    c. Seattle Seahawks
    d. St. Louis Rams

17. Picked by the Colts as the 28th overall pick in the 2000 Draft, Rob Morris was the squad's leading tackler on special teams in 2006. In what state was he born and raised?

    a. Idaho
    b. Illinois
    c. Montana
    d. Wyoming

18. The 29th overall pick in 2005, Marlin Jackson will always be remembered for one play: his pick of Tom Brady as the Colts beat the Pats in the "greatest win" in team history. How many seconds were left on the clock at the time of the pick?

a. 8
b. 18
c. 30
d. 38

19. When Andre Rison broke in as a rookie receiver after being drafted 22nd overall by the Colts in the 1989 Draft, which other receiver did he immediately form a dynamic duo with?

    a. Bill Brooks
    b. Jesse Hester
    c. Brooks Johnson
    d. Zefross Moss

20. Quarterback Jeff George, drafted 1st overall by the Colts in 1990, brought hope to fans far and wide. After an acceptable first year, George and the Colts reeled in his second season. What was their 1991 record?

    a. 1-15
    b. 2-14
    c. 3-13
    d. 5-11

QUIZ ANSWERS

1. C – 1998
2. C – 19th
3. A – True
4. B – Peyton Manning
5. C – Made First Team All-Pro his first two seasons
6. A – Eric Dickerson
7. B – False (Castonzo went to Boston College, not Harvard, and he protected Matt Ryan, not Ryan Fitzpatrick.)
8. D – Rock Ya-Sin, Temple
9. A – 2003
10. C – 110
11. A – Center
12. B – John Elway
13. A – True
14. C – University of Washington
15. A – Jamal Adams of LSU
16. C – Seattle Seahawks
17. A – Idaho
18. B – 18
19. A – Bill Brooks
20. A – 1-15

DID YOU KNOW?

1. When Cornelius O'Landa Bennett was initially drafted by the Colts, he didn't sign. He went to Buffalo for eight years, then Atlanta for three, and finally ended up back in Indy for two more.
2. A 2001 1st round Colts pick, Anthony Castonzo grew up in Hawthorn Woods, IL, where parents Shari and Bill ran an Italian restaurant. He attended Fork Union Military Academy (VA) before Boston College.
3. After Dallas Clark was drafted as a tight end, he helped the Colts to a Super Bowl win. Short stints in Tampa Bay and Baltimore yielded similar results, and he retired before the 2014 season, signing a one-day Colts contract allowing him to retire wearing the horseshoe.
4. Top draftee Steve Emtman only had one regret: "After blowing my ACL, MCL, and patellar tendon (in 1993), I probably wouldn't come back in 11 months. I would have renegotiated with the Colts, stayed out a year, taken a season off, and completely rehabbed. But that's the kind of drive you have as an athlete, to get back on the field."
5. Leonard Coleman came to Indianapolis as the Colts' first pick in the 1985 Draft, 8th overall. However, he sat out the season in a salary dispute and then signed with the USFL's Memphis Showboats.

6. Trev Alberts, drafted 5th overall in 1994, appeared in just five Colts games as a rookie and ended his career with seven starts because of injuries. He'll always be remembered as the player Colts GM Bill Tobin selected instead of Trent Dilfer or Heath Shuler.

7. In 2020, the Colts traded their 1st round draft choice, 13th overall, to acquire defensive tackle DeForest Buckner from San Francisco. Thus, their first pick in the 2021 Draft was number 34.

8. Shane Curry played for some of the best Miami Hurricane teams in college history. He came to the Colts in the 2nd round of the 1991 Draft, started nine games overall, and recorded a single sack.

9. Top draft pick Jeff George played in front of his hometown fans. Unfortunately, he also fought with them, struggled with head coach Ted Marchibroda, and often forgot called plays.

10. At pick number 243 in the 1988 Draft, linebacker Jeff Herrod could be the best Colts selection ever. He once had 22 tackles in a game, 200 in one season, and mustered 1,400 tackles in his career.

CHAPTER 11:

LET'S MAKE A DEAL

QUIZ TIME!

1. When Jeff George refused to join training camp in 1993, the Colts decided to part ways. Which team gave them three future draft picks for George?
    a. Atlanta Falcons
    b. Carolina Panthers
    c. Dallas Cowboys
    d. Detroit Lions
2. In what year was Eric Dickerson involved in a mega-trade among the Colts, Bills, and Rams due to his contract disputes in La-La Land?
    a. 1981
    b. 1984
    c. 1987
    d. 1990
3. How many total draft picks and players did the Colts trade to L.A. in exchange for Dickerson and his dynamic running?

a. 2
b. 4
c. 6
d. 8

4. Along with shipping all the picks they'd received from Buffalo, which running back did the Colts send packing to L.A. to secure Dickerson?

   a. Greg Bell
   b. Owen Gill
   c. Christian Okoye
   d. Walter Payton

5. Which team traded Vontae Davis in 2012 in a swap that turned out heavily in favor of the Colts?

   a. Buffalo Bills
   b. Cincinnati Bengals
   c. Denver Broncos
   d. Miami Dolphins

6. In October 2006, the Colts traded with Tampa Bay for defensive tackle Booger McFarland. At that moment, Indy ranked dead last in league run defense. How many yards per game were they yielding?

   a. 98
   b. 109
   c. 116
   d. 137

7. When the Colts traded away Marshall Faulk in 1999, Edgerrin James was able to fill his spot quite nicely. Who was the Colts' coach at the time?

    a. Jim Caldwell
    b. Rod Dowhower
    c. Jim Mora
    d. Chuck Pagano

8. In 1999, Faulk had missed practices and was pondering holding out for a new contract. Colts President Bill Polian decided that the running back was the odd man out and traded him to the St. Louis Rams in exchange for 2nd and 5th round picks in the upcoming draft.

    a. True
    b. False

9. When John Elway refused to play for the Colts, he was promptly traded to Denver. Which other quarterback came to Indianapolis as part of the trade?

    a. Tony Eason
    b. Mark Hermann
    c. Chris Hinton
    d. Jim Kelly

10. When Ryan Grigson traded a 2014 1st round pick to Cleveland for running back Trent Richardson, he had little idea what the Colts were really getting. How many yards did Trent gain on 157 attempts in 2013?

    a. 367
    b. 458

c. 625
d. 711

11. Which rising star did the Colts swap, along with Chris Hinton and a 5th round pick, to move all the way up to the 1st overall selection in the 1990 Draft?

    a. Pat Beach
    b. Albert Bentley
    c. Ralph Jarvis
    d. Andre Rison

12. In the first major trade in Colts history, in 1953, which of the following players did the franchise NOT acquire?

    a. Harry Agganis
    b. Don Colo
    c. Stew Sheets
    d. Don Shula

13. On January 22, 1973, the Colts decided to trade away legendary quarterback Johnny Unitas for "future considerations" (in other words, cash). How much did they get from the San Diego Chargers?

    a. $80,000
    b. $150,000
    c. $250,000
    d. $500,000

14. Who did the Colts snag from Green Bay in August 1974, who went on to become a star beside Mike Curtis at linebacker, but then retired in 1977 while complaining about being underpaid?

a. Mario Cage
b. John Hadl
c. Ted Hendricks
d. Tom MacLeod

15. In 2003, the Colts used the 5th round pick they received from the Texans to acquire Robert Mathis, a defensive end and linebacker, who starred in the Super Bowl win over Chicago. What job with the franchise did Mathis assume upon retirement in 2016?

    a. Advanced stat analyst
    b. Director of player relations
    c. Official fan greeter
    d. Pass-rush consultant

16. From which team did the Colts acquire three draft picks in 2001, allowing them to secure Reggie Wayne, who now ranks second in franchise history with 1,070 receptions, behind only Marvin Harrison?

    a. Cleveland Browns
    b. Dallas Cowboys
    c. Green Bay Packers
    d. New York Giants

17. When the Colts traded Marshall Faulk to the Rams in 1999, they used one of the draft picks they received to sign linebacker Mike Peterson. In what category did Mike lead the league with 160 in 2000?

    a. Forced fumbles
    b. Interceptions

c. Sacks
d. Tackles

18. In 1994, the Colts dealt with a variety of teams after the Jeff George trade, netting promising linebacker Trev Alberts. Alas, his career was cut short by injury. Which of the following injuries did he NOT sustain?

    a. Concussion
    b. Left shoulder dislocation
    c. Right elbow dislocation
    d. Torn cruciate ligament

19. In the mammoth Eric Dickerson trade, 10 players and draft choices were involved. In NFL history, how many other teams have conducted trades involving more than 10 individuals?

    a. 2
    b. 4
    c. 5
    d. 7

20. How did the *New York Times* describe the trade involving heavyweights Eric Dickerson, Cornelius Bennett, and Greg Bell, among others?

    a. "The trade of the century"
    b. "The trade of the decade"
    c. "The trade that rocked the world"
    d. "The trade to beat all trades"

QUIZ ANSWERS

1. A – Atlanta Falcons
2. C – 1987
3. D – 8
4. B – Owen Gill
5. D – Miami Dolphins
6. C – 116
7. C – Jim Mora
8. A – True
9. B – Mark Hermann
10. B – 458
11. D – Andre Rison
12. B – Don Colo
13. B – $150,000
14. D – Tom MacLeod
15. D – Pass-rush consultant
16. D – New York Giants
17. D – Tackles
18. D – Torn cruciate ligament
19. B – 4
20. B – "The trade of the decade"

DID YOU KNOW?

1. The conditional pick the Colts traded the Falcons for in 1996 became a 1st round draft reality when Jeff George played more than 75% of the snaps in Atlanta in 1995. The pick eventually turned out to be Marvin Harrison.
2. Trading for the pick that brought Harrison set the table for Peyton Manning. Harrison held the single-season record for most receptions with 143 for over ten years before Michael Thomas of the New Orleans Saints broke it in 2019.
3. The mastermind behind the Eric Dickerson blockbuster trade on Halloween in 1987 was Jim Irsay, the 28-year-old GM of the Colts, who also happened to be the son of owner Robert Irsay.
4. Booger McFarland contributed a sack in Super Bowl XLI when the Colts beat the Chicago Bears, 29-17. The second Super Bowl ring of McFarland's career saw the Colts get a second-rounder for a Bowl win.
5. The Marshall Faulk trade paved the way for Manning to make full use of his potential and reach his ceiling. His development laid a foundation that would help the Colts get to the playoffs in 11 of 12 years from 1999 to 2010.
6. After his trade, John Elway became a legend in Denver and set an NFL record for most fourth-quarter comebacks (47) in a career. The Colts got offensive tackle Chris Hinton, who spent seven seasons in Indy.

7. Former Executive of the Year Ryan Grigson made a few boneheaded moves in the trade market that cost him his job at the end of the day. His roster mismanagement appeared to cut Andrew Luck's career short as he retired in 2019 at the age of just 29.
8. Assessing the 1973 Johnny Unitas-for-cash deal the Colts made with the Chargers: Neither team really scored in this exchange. Johnny almost didn't report to the Chargers, and then posted a 1-4 record before retiring after a single season. The Colts reeled in $150K, which didn't go far even back in the '70s.
9. Over the years, the Colts established a trend of making a trade for a pick that was used to bring in an elite receiver. Indy used the 3rd round pick from San Francisco in 2012 to grab T.Y. Hilton, a Florida International standout. He now ranks fourth in franchise history with 552 catches.
10. Undoubtedly, the biggest trade involving the Colts didn't include players, but the franchise itself. Carroll Rosenbloom owned the Baltimore team from 1953 until 1972, when he decided to trade franchises with Robert Irsay.

CHAPTER 12:

WRITING THE RECORD BOOK

QUIZ TIME!

1. Between 2006 and 2020, in what year did the Colts establish a franchise record for the highest season attendance with 535,800?

    a. 2008
    b. 2009
    c. 2010
    d. 2019

2. Peyton Manning was clearly a Colts record-breaker. How many touchdown passes did he toss in his Colts career?

    a. 355
    b. 371
    c. 389
    d. 399

3. Adam Vinatieri booted 1,515 points in his Colts career. How many points did he score in the NFL altogether to rest comfortably ahead of Morten Andersen?

a. 2,544
b. 2,599
c. 2,673
d. 2,812

4. Marvin Harrison ranks first among Colts receivers and ninth all-time (just ahead of Reggie Wayne) in the NFL in receiving yards. Which of the following pass-catchers is NOT ahead of him in the league ranking?

   a. James Lofton
   b. Randy Moss
   c. Terrell Owens
   d. Jerry Rice

5. Johnny Unitas threw more interceptions and had a lower passer rating than Peyton Manning, Andrew Luck, Bert Jones, and Jim Harbaugh. But Johnny U brought three NFL championships and a Super Bowl victory to the Colts franchise.

   a. True
   b. False

6. Although Tony Dungy was the Colts' coach for only seven seasons, he took the team to the playoffs each year. His winning percentage was better than any other coach for the franchise. What was it?

   a. .700
   b. .735
   c. .759
   d. .799

7. Colts owner Irsay had to persuade Dungy to return in 2008 so he could be the head when Lucas Oil Stadium was inaugurated. After a tough 3-4 start, how many straight wins did the team reel off under Dungy that year (before finally being eliminated by San Diego in OT in the playoffs)?
   a. 6
   b. 8
   c. 9
   d. 10
8. When DeForest Buckner terrorized opponents in 2020, which of the following players did he NOT join with at least four tackles, two tackles for a loss, three sacks, and one forced fumble in a single game?
   a. Aaron Donald
   b. Haason Reddick
   c. Justin Houston
   d. Rodrigo Blankenship
9. Buckner continued his rampage by setting a single-season Colts mark for most sacks by a defensive tackle. How many did he rack up?
   a. 5.5
   b. 7.0
   c. 8.5
   d. 9.5
10. Which Colts cornerback became the first since 2013 to return an interception for a touchdown and a blocked punt for a touchdown in the same season?

a. Khari Willis
b. Rock Ya-Sin
c. T.J. Carrie
d. Xavier Rhodes

11. Among several other franchise receiving records he holds, T.Y. Hilton couldn't seem to be stopped by a particular AFC South opponent. Which team allowed Hilton to haul in 100+ yards in each of their eight games?

    a. Baltimore Stallions
    b. Houston Texans
    c. Jacksonville Jaguars
    d. Tennessee Titans

12. In 2020, Nyheim Hines was only the second player in the NFL since 1948 to celebrate his first 100+-yard rushing game together with two or more touchdowns on his birthday. Who was the last to do it in 2005?

    a. Shaun Alexander
    b. Tiki Barber
    c. Samkon Gado
    d. Clinton Portis

13. Justin Houston tied the NFL mark for most career safeties (4) and also became only the fourth defender since 2000 to record two safeties in a season. Which of the following players did NOT tally four career safeties?

    a. Jared Allen
    b. Doug English

c. Ted Hendricks
d. Julius Peppers

14. Also in 2020, Darius Leonard was heralded as the first player in recent NFL history to rack up 300 tackles in his first 30 games. When was the feat last accomplished?

a. 1970
b. 1980
c. 1987
d. 1994

15. Peyton Manning once lit up the Colts' opponents with seven touchdown passes in a single game, tying him with eight other quarterbacks in the annals of the NFL. Sid Luckman was the first to do it, in 1945.

a. True
b. False

16. Bertram Hays Jones, also known as "the Ruston Rifle," was sacked a record number of times (12) in a single game versus the Cards in 1980. That broke the record held by Jones's backup. Who was he?

a. Dan Fouts
b. Greg Landry
c. Warren Moon
d. Joe Theisman

17. In the Colts' Super Bowl XLI victory, Joseph Addai caught a record number of passes for a running back in the ultimate game. How many?

a. 8
b. 10
c. 12
d. 15

18. In a list of NFL records that will "never" be broken, Marvin Harrison's 143 receptions in the 2002 season stands tall. The next closest receiver that season had 31 fewer catches. Who was that?

    a. Plaxico Burress
    b. Donald Driver
    c. Peerless Price
    d. Hines Ward

19. The 2004 Colts squad broke numerous records, including the number of touchdown passes (a historic NFL mark) and total points in a season (522—the best in the NFL that season). How many touchdown passes did they rack up that year?

    a. 57
    b. 51
    c. 45
    d. 40

20. In December 2009, the Colts broke the NFL record for consecutive wins as they maintained their perfect season at 13-0. Whose record did they shatter with their 22nd straight win?

    a. Chicago Bears
    b. Denver Broncos
    c. New England Patriots
    d. Seattle Seahawks

QUIZ ANSWERS

1. C – 2010
2. D – 399
3. C – 2,673
4. A – James Lofton
5. A – True
6. C – .759
7. C – 9
8. D – Rodrigo Blankenship
9. D – 9.5
10. C – T.J. Carrie
11. B – Houston Texans
12. C – Samkon Gado
13. D – Julius Peppers
14. C – 1987
15. B – False (Sid Luckman first did the daring deed in 1943, not 1945.)
16. B – Greg Landry
17. B – 10
18. D – Hines Ward
19. B – 51
20. C – New England Patriots

DID YOU KNOW?

1. When Colts quarterback Peyton Manning inked a landmark $99.2 million, seven-year contract that would pay him a league-record $14.17 million annually, he said simply, "I'm happy to be a Colt for life." Manning later moved, concluding his sterling career with the Denver Broncos.
2. The NFL record for sacks in a 16-game season is 22.5, set by Michael Strahan of the New York Giants in 2001. The Baltimore coaching staff once reviewed a season's worth of film and counted 43 sacks by Gino Marchetti in a 12-game season. He once had nine sacks in a single game.
3. After 33 seasons as an NFL head coach, Don Shula retired following the 1995 season. His regular-season record of 328-156-6, together with a 19-17 post-season mark, gave the legendary coach a career total of 347 wins, 173 losses, and six ties.
4. When Colts President and Treasurer Robert Irsay finally decided in 1984 that the franchise wouldn't survive in Baltimore, he struck a deal with the city of Indianapolis, jammed all the team's equipment in fifteen semi-trucks, and drove them to Indy overnight.
5. While not exactly a record, the so-called "Colts Catastrophe" was an attempt at a trick play against the Patriots in 2015. The botched fake punt resulted not only in a tackle for a loss,

but a penalty, a distasteful defeat against a major rival, and complete criticism of the Colts players and coaches who messed it up.

6. As they cranked up their record-breaking offense in the 2004 campaign, the Colts scored more points (277) in the first halves of their games than seven other NFL teams managed to score in the entire season.
7. The Colts broke yet another long-standing record in December 2009, notching their 114th win of the decade and breaking a tie with the San Francisco 49ers of the 1990s. Indy also broke a franchise record with their 13th straight win at home.
8. During the 2014 season, Andrew Luck aired it out for 4,761 yards, eclipsing the franchise record of 4,700 yards that Peyton Manning had established in the 2010 campaign.
9. In his first six seasons as a Colt, Luck ranked in the top five in NFL history in both the number of touchdown passes he threw (171) and total yards passing (23,671). In the former category, Andrew trailed only Hall-of-Famer Dan Marino's 196 touchdown strikes in the first six seasons of his career.
10. Following his 2016 shoulder surgery, Luck remained out of action for 616 days until his next start. He came blasting back with a career-high 67.3% completion rate and 98.7 passer rating to cop the 2018 Comeback Player of the Year Award.

CHAPTER 13:

BRING ON THE RIVALS

QUIZ TIME!

1. At the end of the 2020 season, the dreaded New England Patriots had an edge in their historical rivalry against the Colts. What was the advantage?
    a. 41-40
    b. 42-39
    c. 45-36
    d. 52-29
2. The two narrowest victories in the long rivalry were both by the Colts over the Patriots: 29-28 and 35-34. When was the most recent of these squeakers?
    a. 1981
    b. 1999
    c. 2004
    d. 2009
3. This modern rivalry really heated up when quarterbacks Peyton Manning and Tom Brady battled each other for

supremacy from 2001 through 2011. Who did Brady replace in his first start against the Colts?

a. Drew Bledsoe
b. Matt Cassel
c. Tony Eason
d. Steve Grogan

4. In the November 2009 game between the two bitter rivals, New England coach Belichick decided to go for it all on fourth down and two, and the Pats failed. Manning came right back to Wayne for a score, and the Colts' kicker drilled the PAT for a 35-34 win. Who was the kicker that day?

    a. Bucky Dilts
    b. Lou Michaels
    c. Matt Stover
    d. Adam Vinatieri

5. Which team vehemently opposed the Colts' reentry to the league in 1953 and thus became rivals in the 1950s, principally due to geography?

    a. New York Giants
    b. New York Jets
    c. Philadelphia Eagles
    d. Washington Redskins

6. In the so-called "Greatest Game Ever Played" between the Colts and the Giants in 1958, which famous coach (then with the Giants) was strutting the sidelines in his final game as offensive coordinator?

a. Jim Lee Howell
b. Vince Lombardi
c. Bill Parcells
d. Earl Potteiger

7. The Colts now face off against several rivals in the AFC South division. What team did the Tennessee Titans originate from?

   a. Dallas Texans
   b. Houston Oilers
   c. Kansas City Renegades
   d. Los Angeles Chargers

8. The Colts' Super Bowl XLI win in 2006 is the only Super Bowl victory by an AFC South team to date, and the division boasts the longest active Super Bowl victory drought.

   a. True
   b. False

9. When the Colts were led by Andrew Luck, which team became a "thorn in their side," blocking them from the playoffs in both 2015 and 2016?

   a. Houston Texans
   b. Jacksonville Jaguars
   c. New Orleans Saints
   d. Tennessee Titans

10. If the Houston Texans are really to be considered serious rivals of the Colts, they need to improve on their head-to-head results. What advantage did the Colts hold in the series as of 2020?

a. 29-9
b. 25-12
c. 22-15
d. 20-17

11. When Tony Dungy was chosen to work on NBC's *Football Night in America,* there was concern that he might not be able to get along on the program with a rival safety Tony had coached against. Who was the hitman?

 a. Rodney Harrison, Patriots
 b. Troy Polamalu, Steelers
 c. Adrian Wilson, Cardinals
 d. Rod Woodson, Raiders

12. Which of the following rivalries is NOT mentioned in the same breath as the Colts versus the Patriots in terms of all-time NFL battles?

 a. Chiefs vs. Raiders
 b. Cowboys vs. Giants
 c. Seahawks vs. Chargers
 d. Steelers vs. Browns

13. Fanning the fire in 2008, New England's Belichick indirectly questioned Tony Dungy's honesty. Related to what?

 a. The exact pressure used in Indy's footballs
 b. The Indy injury report
 c. Indy player numbers
 d. Whether Indy had used cameras to spy on Patriots' practices

14. In a 2010 article on NFL coaching feuds, the tense faceoff between Dungy and Belichick was ranked as the fourth worst in history. Which of the following was voted the worst?

    a. George Allen and Tom Landry
    b. Bill Belichick and Eric Mangini
    c. Mike Ditka and Buddy Ryan
    d. Mike Shanahan and Al Davis

15. Early in 2007, this was written about the Colts: "As great a coach as he is—Dungy has won 63 games in the past five seasons—he has failed to reach the Super Bowl. And Manning, who is closing in on his 31st birthday, is still trying to avoid joining Dan Fouts and Warren Moon as the greatest quarterbacks during the Super Bowl era never to have played in the game."

    a. True
    b. False

16. When the Colts finally qualified to host the 2007 AFC Championship Game against the rival Patriots, they would at least be able to avoid the ______ January conditions in Foxboro Stadium, according to the *Sun Sentinel*. What word is missing?

    a. Frigid
    b. Horrific
    c. Hostile
    d. Unreal

17. In a 2003 home playoff game for Indianapolis, which Patriots' player contributed a last-minute goal-line tackle to stymie the Colts' best-ever running back, Edgerrin James, as well as their high-powered offense?

    a. Dyshod Carter
    b. Je'Rod Cherry
    c. Ty Law
    d. Willie McGinest

18. "I think the fans here are great. They love their team. They get a few jabs at the opposing team's bench, which is what you get everywhere. It's always fun to come and play here. You're playing a good team, in a great stadium, with great fans." Which opposing quarterback said this about Colts fans?

    a. Tom Brady
    b. Patrick Mahomes
    c. Philip Rivers
    d. Ben Roethlisberger

19. A Colts coach once said this about facing the Pats: "I do know for a fact that it was always a 60-minute chess match. It has ever-changing looks and disguises, and they always tend to find ways to figure out some of your signals." Who made this accusation?

    a. Marcus Brady
    b. Matt Eberflus
    c. Pep Hamilton
    d. Bubba Ventrone

20. When the Patriots beat the Colts in the 2014 AFC Championship Game, what was the name soon given to the controversy that swirled around the matchup?

  a. Debategate
  b. Deflategate
  c. Spygate
  d. Watergate

QUIZ ANSWERS

1. D – 52-29
2. D – 2009
3. A – Drew Bledsoe
4. C – Matt Stover
5. D – Washington Redskins
6. B – Vince Lombardi
7. B – Houston Oilers
8. A – True
9. A – Houston Texans
10. A – 29-9
11. A – Rodney Harrison, Patriots
12. C – Seahawks vs. Chargers
13. B – The Indy injury report
14. C – Mike Ditka and Buddy Ryan
15. A – True
16. A – Frigid
17. D – Willie McGinest
18. C – Philip Rivers
19. C – Pep Hamilton
20. B – Deflategate

DID YOU KNOW?

1. Considered one of the most famous rivalries in the NFL, the Colts and the Patriots have combined for seven Super Bowl victories (six by the Pats) and eleven AFC Championships (nine by the Pats) since 2001. Both franchises are recognized for their organizational excellence.
2. Though the two teams were initially rivals in the East dating back to the time the Colts were in Baltimore, their intensified enmity was not truly felt until Indianapolis moved into the newly formed AFC South after 2001 as part of the NFL's realignment.
3. The Colts moved to Indianapolis in 1970, and the Washington Redskins almost moved to Louisville, Kentucky, due to low attendance at their games in the nation's capital.
4. In the history of the NFL, the best football between two teams for a sustained period of time was played when the Baltimore Colts and the Green Bay Packers butted heads between 1959 and 1967. Every one of their games eventually decided who would win the NFL championship that season, and each of their contests from 1962 to 1967 was televised nationally.
5. According to one local writer, the only thing that keeps Houston from becoming as big a rival as the Pats is that the Texans' fans and players aren't "inherently unlikable in the same way that Patriots fans and players are."

6. It's hard to give your toughest rivals due credit. When Tony Dungy was asked if Tom Brady was the most difficult rival quarterback to stop in NFL history, he ranked him only sixth behind the likes of John Elway, Aaron Rodgers, and Steve Young, because of the running abilities of those quarterbacks.

7. Tony was also tough on rival coach Belichick when he said, "I don't think Bill Belichick would be Bill Belichick without Tom Brady and Brady would not have the same success without Belichick and the way they have put that team together."

8. Dungy and ex-rival Rodney Harrison were teamed up on NBC. Harrison admitted, "I didn't know him well before we were put together. I didn't know what to expect. He was the enemy. Coach (Dungy) was the enemy. He was a part of the whole Peyton Manning-vs.-the-Patriots thing. We had a lot of respect for the coach but we didn't like him and we wanted to beat him." Harrison concluded that Belichick and Dungy were the two smartest people he ever met in football.

9. But even in the TV booth, Dungy and Harrison continued to be rivals of sorts. "Rodney still thinks like a player, and I still think like a coach," Dungy quipped. "So we still have those disputes on the show."

10. Although the Colts and Steelers have battled each other for AFC supremacy for years, Pittsburgh pundits don't consider the Colts as one of their "Top 10" foes.

CONCLUSION

If we've done our job well, you've reached this point chock-full of new facts about your favorite NFL team, the Indianapolis Colts. Whether it's the notable players who hold franchise records or some of the behind-the-scenes information about how some of your favorite stars arrived in Indy, we hope you enjoyed this trip down memory lane and through the rich history of the Colts.

We've done our best to cover it all for you, from the joys of the 1958 and 1959 seasons to Super Bowl victories in 1971 and 2007, in addition to some of the darker days in the franchise's history.

In the Super Bowl era, Indianapolis has had its fair share of highlights, but there have been some lean years in the Crossroads of America as well. Throughout the Colts' storied history, some of the best players to ever play the game have done so with the franchise—first in Baltimore and later in Indianapolis. They might not have as many Lombardi Trophies as you'd like, but the Colts are a large part of the fabric of the league we know and love.

This book is designed for you, the fans, to embrace your favorite team and feel closer to it. Maybe you weren't totally familiar with franchise history. Perhaps you were unaware of the early success the Colts had in the NFL. Maybe you didn't realize just how shrewdly the Colts used and traded their draft picks to pick up legendary talents.

Or perhaps we couldn't stump you at all, and you're the ultimate super-fan! No matter how well you did on the quizzes, we hope we captured the spirit of the Colts and inspired even more pride for your team.

The Colts are still one of the winningest teams in league history, and, as always, they'll continue to give it their all. "Go Horse!" "Do the Blue!" We're still working on a great new catch phrase for next year.

Stay tuned!

Printed in Great Britain
by Amazon

14374654R00078